DISCOVERING FISH

by Charis Mather

Minneapolis, Minnesota

Credits
All images are courtesy of Shutterstock.com, unless otherwise specified. With thanks to Getty Images, Thinkstock Photo, and iStockphoto. Recurring – Net Vector, Baskiabat, NotionPic, PCH.Vector, Latelier, Susann Guenther. Cover – Andrea Izzotti, Marina Yesina, Dennis Forster. 2–3 – Shayne Meyers Photography. 4–5 – carlos castilla. 6–7 – Andrei Armiagov, Colorcocktail, Damsea. 8–9 – Andrea Izzotti, Jason LSL. 10–11 – kaschibo. 12–13 – Image Source Trading Ltd, wildestanimal. 14–15 – Sean Steininger, Dennis Forster, Andrea Izzotti. 16–17 – Mark Subscenic Harris, Martin Voeller. 18–19 – L.T. Southall, Vladimir Turkenich. 20–21 – eshoot, Ian Scott, kaschibo, Solarisys, Vitaly Korovin, Vlad61. 22–23 – jakkapan, Romolo Tavani.

Bearport Publishing Company Product Development Team
Publisher: Jen Jenson; Director of Product Development: Spencer Brinker; Managing Editor: Allison Juda; Editor: Cole Nelson; Associate Editor: Tiana Tran; Production Editor: Naomi Reich; Designer: Kim Jones; Designer: Kayla Eggert; Designer: Steve Scheluchin; Production Specialist: Owen Hamlin

Library of Congress Cataloging-in-Publication Data is available at www.loc.gov or upon request from the publisher.

ISBN: 979-8-89577-024-5 (hardcover)
ISBN: 979-8-89577-455-7 (paperback)
ISBN: 979-8-89577-141-9 (ebook)

© 2026 BookLife Publishing
This edition is published by arrangement with BookLife Publishing.

North American adaptations © 2026 Bearport Publishing Company. All rights reserved. No part of this publication may be reproduced in whole or in part, stored in any retrieval system, or transmitted in any form or by any means, electronic, mechanical, photocopying, recording, or otherwise, without written permission from the publisher. Bearport Publishing is a division of FlutterBee Education Group.

For more information, write to Bearport Publishing, 3500 American Blvd W, Suite 150, Bloomington, MN 55431.

CONTENTS

All Aboard! 4
For Your Information . . .6
Sharks 8
Pilot Fish 10
Sailfish 12
Sardines 14
Ocean Sunfish 16
Flying Fish. 18
Coral Reef Fish. 20
Back on Land! 22
Glossary 24
Index 24

ALL ABOARD!

Ahoy there! Welcome aboard my ship. I am Captain Gulliver of the See-Gulls Ocean Tours. My crew and I are happy to have you along for our journey.

FOR YOUR INFORMATION

The ocean is home to a lot of fish. In fact, there are about 20,000 different kinds! They come in many shapes, sizes, and colors.

The ocean is a fishy feast for seagulls like me!

Many fish live near the ocean's **surface**. The water there is warmer and gets more light than down below. Some of these fish are found near coasts and in **coral reefs**. Others swim in the open ocean.

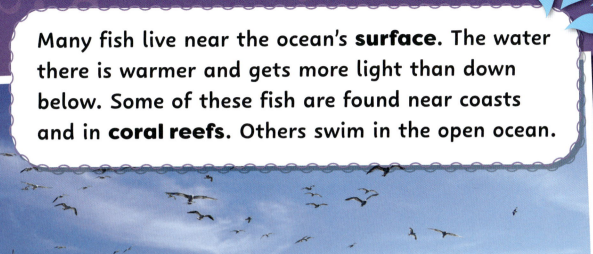

The ocean has different layers. The layer closest to the surface is called the sunlight zone.

SHARKS

Sharks spotted!

The largest fish in the ocean are whale sharks. Despite their size, they are not **dangerous** to humans (or seagulls). Whale sharks eat mostly tiny ocean creatures, such as shrimp.

A WHALE SHARK

All sharks have bendy skeletons that allow them to swim quickly.

Many kinds of sharks are not gentle. Great white sharks are fierce **predators**. They have powerful jaws and hundreds of sharp teeth. Great whites use their mouths to rip **prey** into bite-sized chunks.

A GREAT WHITE SHARK

Let's stay away from great white sharks!

PILOT FISH

Pilot fish are often found swimming near sharks. However, they don't usually become shark food. This is because pilot fish help keep sharks healthy. These fish eat **parasites** off the bodies of the larger fish.

Pilot fish have blue and silver stripes on their bodies.

PILOT FISH

10

Pilot fish also chow down on leftovers. They eat the scraps of food that sharks leave behind. Sometimes, they follow ships and fishing boats, hoping to get any food tossed overboard.

Don't be surprised if pilot fish start following our boat!

SAILFISH

Is that a fish or a boat?

You have to be quick to spot a sailfish speeding through the water. These fish are some of the fastest in the ocean. They can reach speeds of about 70 miles per hour (110 kph).

Sailfish get their name from the large, sail-like fins on their backs.

Sailfish use their speed to hunt smaller fish, such as sardines. Sometimes, they work together to catch their food. Sailfish circle their prey, gathering them into a group. Then, the speedy fish attack.

Sailfish can also launch themselves out of the water at high speeds.

SARDINES

Sardines have silvery bodies and can grow to be 12 inches (30 cm) long. They usually live together in large groups called schools.

Sardines eat mostly tiny animals called zooplankton.

Once a year, millions of sardines group together to travel a long distance. This is called a sardine run. Often, the sardine run is so big that it can be seen from space.

During the run, many sardines are eaten by predators.

It looks like we'll have a big lunch today!

OCEAN SUNFISH

Ocean sunfish have large, flat bodies. They spend a lot of time near the surface, soaking up sunlight to stay warm. However, they sometimes dive deep to find jellyfish to eat.

Ocean sunfish don't have tail fins. This has earned them the nickname headfish.

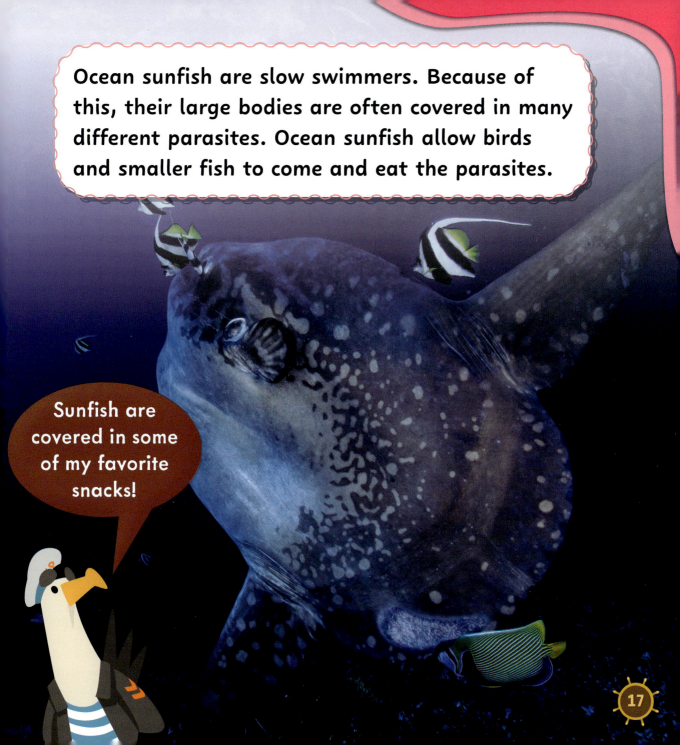

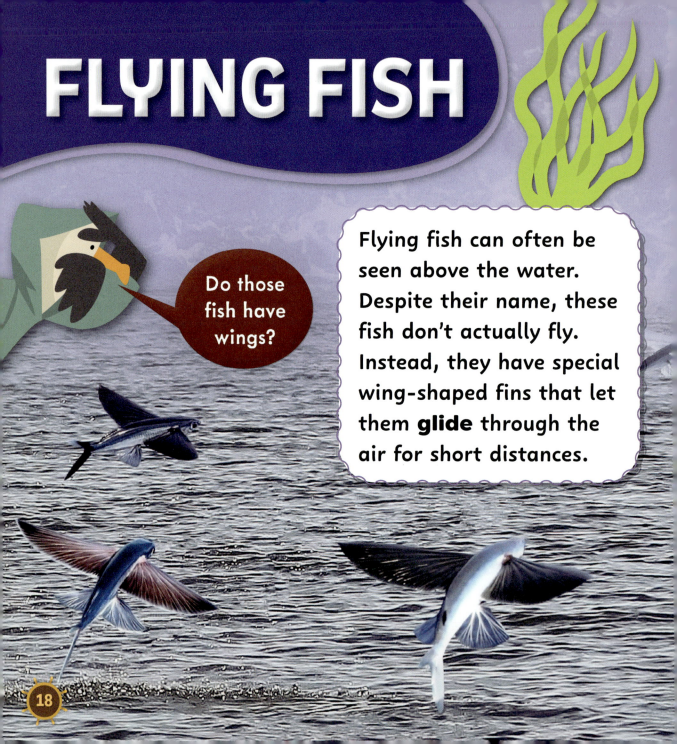

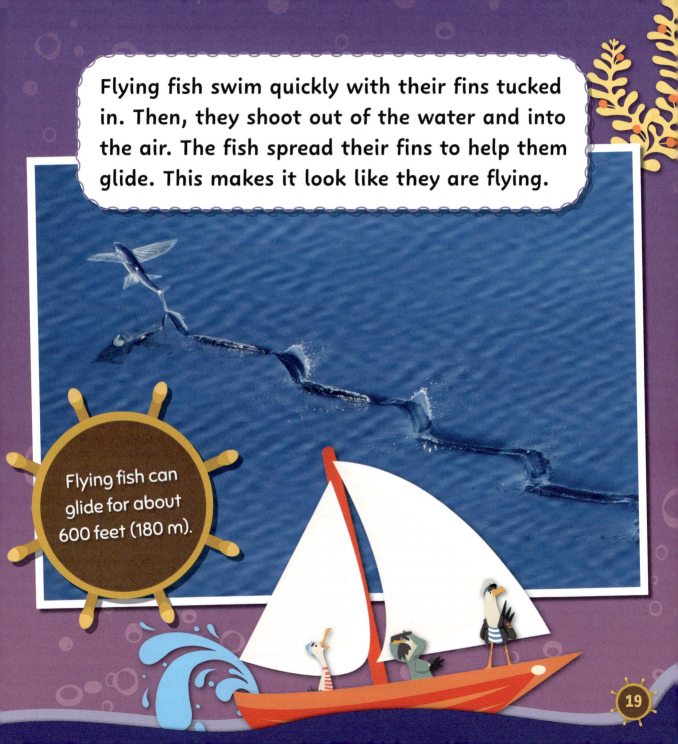

Flying fish swim quickly with their fins tucked in. Then, they shoot out of the water and into the air. The fish spread their fins to help them glide. This makes it look like they are flying.

Flying fish can glide for about 600 feet (180 m).

CORAL REEF FISH

Let's take a look at a warm and colorful coral reef! This **habitat** has more types of fish in one place than any other part of the ocean.

A CORAL REEF

More than 4,000 different kinds of fish live in coral reefs.

Many fish that live in coral reefs are colorful. This helps them hide from predators. The fish easily blend in with the bright corals.

ROYAL ANGELFISH

MOORISH IDOL

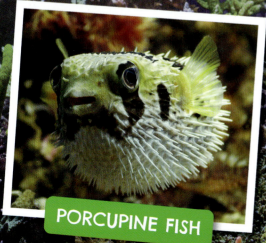

PORCUPINE FISH

YELLOW BOXFISH

BACK ON LAND!

That is all the sightseeing we have time for today. Let's head back to land. We hope you enjoyed learning about some of the wonderful fish in the ocean!

Land, ho!

GLOSSARY

coral reefs rocklike structures formed from the bodies of sea animals called polyps

dangerous likely to cause harm

glide to move in the air smoothly without flapping

habitat a place in nature where plants and animals live

parasites creatures that live on or in other living things and harm them

predators animals that hunt and eat other animals

prey animals that are hunted and eaten by other animals

surface the top of the water

INDEX

birds 17
color 6, 20–21
coral 7, 20–21
fins 12, 16, 18–19
flying 18–19
food 10–11, 13
parasites 10, 17
predators 9, 15, 21
prey 9, 13
skeleton 8
teeth 9